WOULD YOU LIKE FREE RESOURCES?

EMAIL "FREE" TO DECODABLETEXTS@GMAIL.COM TO SIGN UP FOR OUR NEWSLETTER AND RECEIVE FREE RESOURCES.

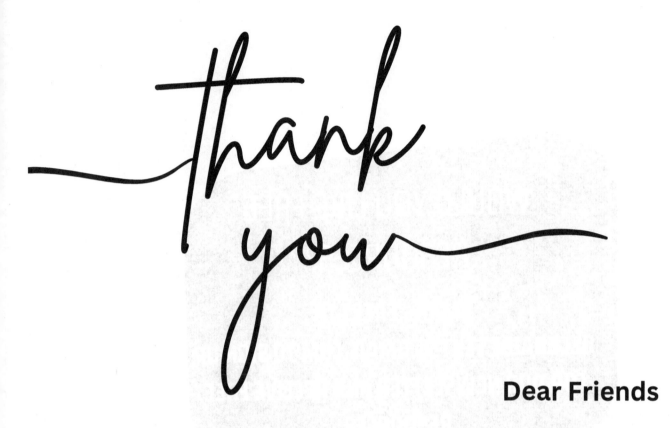

Dear Friends

Thank you for choosing our reading test grade 5 and 6 workbook. I hope that this book serves you and your family well. If you have found value in this book, please consider leaving us a review on amazon. It would be very much appreciated.

Adam Freeman

Text 1

Annotation Checklist

As you read the text, please annotate it using the following checklist:

 Underline any main ideas

 Circle any words you don't know

 Look up the words online

 Reread anything you don't understand

 Summarize after rereading

 Write Down things you find interesting

 yes!

Note Taking

The Industrial Revolution: Gears, Gadgets, and Giggles

Introduction: Factories, Trains, and... Computers?

Whoa! Hold onto your top hats, kids! The Industrial Revolution wasn't just about smoke and machines. It was a time of massive change, affecting how people worked, traveled, and even how they spent their weekends. Imagine a world without your favorite video games or mobile devices. That's right, before the Industrial Revolution, things were very different.

While the Industrial Revolution started around the late 18th century, its impact has continued to this day. Think of it as the great-granddaddy of all the cool tech stuff you have now. So, before you jet off on your electric scooters or tap away on your tablets, let's dive deep into this exciting era.

Spinning a Yarn: The Textile Industry's Makeover

Do you fancy wearing potato sacks instead of cool t-shirts? Well, thanks to the Industrial Revolution, you don't have to! Before this period, making clothes was a super slow process. People spun threads and wove fabrics by hand. But then, along came inventions like the spinning jenny and the power loom. These machines could do the work of many people in less time.

The textile industry was among the first to be transformed. Faster production meant more clothes and, guess what? Lower prices! So, while today you might be hunting for the latest sneaker drop, back then, people were just thrilled to get socks that didn't cost a fortune.

Going Loco with Locomotives: The Rise of Railways
Choo-Choo! All aboard the train of progress! Before trains, traveling from one city to another was a bumpy and dusty ordeal on horseback or in carriages. But the invention of the steam engine changed everything. Suddenly, people could cover distances in hours instead of days.

The railways didn't just make travel faster. They also connected people from different parts of the country. Products and goods could be transported quickly, leading to the growth of businesses. Plus, with the railroads, people could now take vacations to distant places. Beach trip, anyone?

Machines & Mankind: The Good, the Bad, and the Ugly
Machines are awesome, right? But every coin has two sides. As factories grew, they needed more workers. Many people moved from the countryside to cities in search of jobs. This sudden growth led to crowded living conditions, and not all of it was pleasant.

On the bright side, machines made many tasks easier and production faster. But, they also posed challenges. People had to work long hours in sometimes unsafe conditions. Over time, this led to the creation of laws to protect workers. So, while the Industrial Revolution brought cool gadgets, it also taught society the importance of fairness and safety.

Echoes of the Past: The Revolution's Impact Today
Sure, the Industrial Revolution happened a long time ago, but its effects still ripple through today. Many of the technologies and industries that started back then have paved the way for the cool stuff we have today. Imagine if there were no trains – how would you travel for your summer vacations?

From the computers we use to the cars we drive, traces of the Industrial Revolution are everywhere. It was a time of creativity and growth that helped shape the world in countless ways. And while the machines of that era might seem old-fashioned, they were the starting point for the modern wonders we enjoy now.

1. Which section talks about the challenges faced by workers during the Industrial Revolution?
    - A) 1
    - B) 2
    - C) 3
    - D) 4
2. What is the main idea of the section titled "Spinning a Yarn: The Textile Industry's Makeover"?
    - A) Clothes became cheaper.
    - B) The textile industry was transformed by machines.
    - C) Socks became affordable.
    - D) Handmade clothes were better.
3. Which detail supports the idea that the railways connected people?
    - A) Trains made selling goods easier.
    - B) Steam engines changed everything.
    - C) Products could be transported quickly.
    - D) People could take vacations to distant places.
4. What does the word "loco" in the heading "Going Loco with Locomotives" most likely mean?
    - A) Local
    - B) Crazy
    - C) Location
    - D) Loud
5. Who is the author's intended audience for this text?
    - A) Factory owners from the 1800s
    - B) University professors
    - C) Train conductors
    - D) Kids learning about the Industrial Revolution

6. In your own words, describe the tone the author uses in the text.

_____

_____

_____

_____

7. How did the growth of the textile industry impact consumers? Provide evidence from the text.

_____

_____

_____

_____

8. According to the text, why were laws eventually created during the Industrial Revolution?

_____

_____

_____

_____

Write a short essay discussing the lasting impact of the Industrial Revolution on today's world, using information from the "Echoes of the Past: The Revolution's Impact Today" section.

_____

_____

_____

_____

_____

_____

_____

_____

_____

_____

_____

_____

_____

_____

_____

_____

Answer key

1. Which section talks about the challenges faced by workers during the Industrial Revolution?
    - A) 1
    - B) 2
    - C) 3
    - D) 4
2. What is the main idea of the section titled "Spinning a Yarn: The Textile Industry's Makeover"?
    - A) Clothes became cheaper.
    - B) The textile industry was transformed by machines.
    - C) Socks became affordable.
    - D) Handmade clothes were better.
3. Which detail supports the idea that the railways connected people?
    - A) Trains made selling goods easier.
    - B) Steam engines changed everything for travelers.
    - C) Products could be transported quickly.
    - D) People could take vacations to distant places.
4. What does the word "loco" in the heading "Going Loco with Locomotives" most likely mean?
    - A) Local
    - B) Crazy
    - C) Location
    - D) Loud
5. Who is the author's intended audience for this text?
    - A) Factory owners from the 1800s
    - B) University professors
    - C) Train conductors
    - D) Kids learning about the Industrial Revolution

Text 2

Annotation Checklist

As you read the text, please annotate it using the following checklist:

 Underline any main ideas

 Circle any words you don't know

 Look up the words online

 Reread anything you don't understand

 Summarize after rereading

 Write Down things you find interesting

Note Taking

Name: _____

Date: _____

The Civil Rights Movement: Heroes, Hurdles, and Hope

Introduction: What Are Civil Rights, Anyway?
Hey, future world-changers! Have you ever wondered why we have laws to make sure everyone is treated fairly? Well, it wasn't always this way. In fact, there was a time in the United States when not everyone was given the same rights. Civil rights are the freedoms and rights that everybody should have, no matter their skin color, where they come from, or what they believe.

The Civil Rights Movement was a super important time during the 1950s and 1960s. Brave men and women stood up against unfair treatment and fought for equality. It was a time of big speeches, peaceful marches, and courageous actions. So, buckle up! We're about to take a ride through history!

No More Standing in the Back: The Fight for Fair Treatment
Imagine having to drink from a separate water fountain or sit in a different part of the bus just because of how you look. Sounds unfair, right? Well, that's exactly what was happening. African Americans were not allowed to go to the same schools, eat in the same restaurants, or even use the same bathrooms as white people.

Heroes like Rosa Parks, known as the "mother of the civil rights movement," made a huge difference. She refused to give up her seat to a white person on a bus. Can you believe she got arrested for that? Her brave action started a big bus boycott and helped ignite the movement.

Speaking Up: The Power of Words and Peaceful Protests
Would you stand in front of thousands of people and give a speech? Sounds scary, huh? Martin Luther King Jr., a leader in the movement, did exactly that. He believed in using words, not fists. He had a dream that his children would one day live in a nation where they wouldn't be judged by their skin color but by their character.

People organized sit-ins, where they'd sit in places they weren't allowed and refuse to leave. They did peaceful marches, like the famous one in Washington, D.C., where Dr. King gave his "I Have a Dream" speech. These actions were peaceful, but they were so powerful they helped change laws!

Tough Times and Big Changes: The Movement's Impact
Okay, here's the tough part. Standing up for what's right wasn't easy. People in the movement were often treated harshly. They were arrested, sprayed with water hoses, and sometimes even attacked by dogs. It was dangerous, but they kept going because they believed in justice and equality.

Because of their hard work and sacrifice, big changes happened. Laws were passed, like the Civil Rights Act of 1964, which made it illegal to treat people differently based on their race, color, religion, sex, or national origin. Schools were desegregated, meaning kids of all races could learn together. It was a huge step toward fairness!

Echoes of Courage: The Movement's Legacy Today
The Civil Rights Movement might seem like ancient history from your grandparents' time, but its spirit is still alive today! The bravery and speeches from those days continue to inspire people all over the world to stand up against unfairness.

Thanks to the movement, there are laws that protect civil rights, making sure schools and workplaces are fair. But the fight for equality isn't over. People continue to work hard to make sure everyone, no matter who they are, gets a fair chance. The heroes of the Civil Rights Movement taught us that even when things get tough, never give up on fighting for what's right!

1. According to the text, why was Rosa Parks arrested?
    - A) For making a speech
    - B) For refusing to give up her bus seat
    - C) For organizing a march
    - D) For attending school
2. What is the main idea of the section titled "Speaking Up: The Power of Words and Peaceful Protests"?
    - A) People used violent methods to achieve civil rights.
    - B) Only speeches were used to protest for civil rights.
    - C) The Civil Rights Movement was led solely by Martin Luther King Jr.
    - D) Peaceful protests and powerful words were significant tools in the Civil Rights Movement.\
3. Which detail from the text supports the idea that the Civil Rights Movement faced serious challenges?
    - A) People were inspired by big speeches.
    - B) The movement led to new laws.
    - C) Protesters were often treated harshly.
    - D) Schools were desegregated.
4. What does the word "desegregated" most likely mean in the context where it is used?
    - A) Separated based on race
    - B) Mixed together regardless of race
    - C) Given less importance
    - D) Treated with disrespect
5. Who is the author's intended audience for this text?
    - A) Historians studying the Civil Rights Movement
    - B) Adults who participated in the Civil Rights Movement
    - C) Kids learning about the Civil Rights Movement
    - D) Lawmakers creating civil rights policies

6. How does the author feel about the heroes of the
Civil Rights Movement, based on the text?

_____

_____

_____

_____

7. What changes occurred because of the Civil Rights
Movement? Provide evidence from the text.

_____

_____

_____

_____

8. What were some ways people in the Civil Rights
Movement protested for their rights?

_____

_____

_____

_____

Write a short essay about how the actions of individuals like Rosa Parks and Martin Luther King Jr. contributed to the goals of the Civil Rights Movement, using information from the text.

_____

_____

_____

_____

_____

_____

_____

_____

_____

_____

_____

_____

_____

_____

_____

_____

_____

_____

Answer key

1. According to the text, why was Rosa Parks arrested?
     - A) For making a speech
     - B) For refusing to give up her bus seat
     - C) For organizing a march
     - D) For attending school
2. What is the main idea of the section titled "Speaking Up: The Power of Words and Peaceful Protests"?
     - A) People used violent methods to achieve civil rights.
     - B) Only speeches were used to protest for civil rights.
     - C) The Civil Rights Movement was led solely by Martin Luther King Jr.
     - D) Peaceful protests and powerful words were significant tools in the Civil Rights Movement.
3. Which detail from the text supports the idea that the Civil Rights Movement faced serious challenges?
     - A) People were inspired by big speeches.
     - B) The movement led to new laws.
     - C) Protesters were often treated harshly.
     - D) Schools were desegregated.
4. What does the word "desegregated" most likely mean in the context where it is used?
     - A) Separated based on race
     - B) Mixed together regardless of race
     - C) Given less importance
     - D) Treated with disrespect
5. Who is the author's intended audience for this text?
     - A) Historians studying the Civil Rights Movement
     - B) Adults who participated in the Civil Rights Movement
     - C) Kids learning about the Civil Rights Movement
     - D) Lawmakers creating civil rights policies

Text 3

Annotation Checklist

As you read the text, please annotate it using the following checklist:

- ✓ Underline any main ideas
- ✓ Circle any words you don't know
- ✓ Look up the words online
- ✓ Reread anything you don't understand
- ✓ Summarize after rereading
- ✓ Write Down things you find interesting

yes!

Note Taking

Cultural Festivals: A World of Color, Joy, and Tasty Treats!

Introduction: What's a Cultural Festival?

Hey, young explorers! Ever dressed up in a costume, danced like nobody's watching, or tasted a dish so strange but yummy you couldn't stop eating? If so, you've touched the tip of the iceberg of what cultural festivals are all about! These are events that communities celebrate to honor their unique traditions, histories, or religious milestones – and they do it with a splash of style!

Cultural festivals happen all around the world, offering a rainbow of activities that include parades, dances, music, and, yes, loads of exotic foods. So, slap on your adventure hats, because we're about to embark on a global festival tour without leaving your reading spot!

Lanterns in the Sky: The Magical Mid-Autumn Festival

Let's jet off to China and some other Asian countries, where the Mid-Autumn Festival lights up the night sky! Falling on the 15th day of the 8th month according to the lunar calendar, this festival is a visual treat. Families come together to watch the full moon, light lanterns, and eat mooncakes. The mooncakes are round like the full moon, symbolizing unity and happiness. Kids can be seen running around with brightly-lit, colorful lanterns, making the night shimmer with magic.

Colors Everywhere: The Vibrant Holi Festival

Next stop: India! In this country, there's a festival that looks like a rainbow exploded! Holi, also known as the Festival of Colors, celebrates the victory of good over evil and the arrival of spring. Imagine a giant, joyful water fight, but with colors! People throw powdery, vibrant colors on each other and dance to music, followed by sharing mouth-watering treats. It's not just fun; it also symbolizes putting past troubles behind, good beating evil, and making friends with everyone—even strangers!

Spooky But Sweet: The Unique Day of the Dead

Now, heading over to Mexico, we find a festival that might sound spooky but is actually a sweet remembrance of loved ones who have passed away. Día de los Muertos, or Day of the Dead, isn't your typical festival. Families make altars decorated with marigolds, photos, candles, and favorite foods of their departed loved ones to invite them back for a visit. It's a beautiful mix of sadness and joy, showing that love doesn't end with memory.

Samba in the Streets: The Energetic Rio Carnival

Last on our journey is the Rio Carnival in Brazil, known as one of the biggest parties on Earth! For five days before the calm of Lent (a religious period of simplicity), the city explodes into a festival of dance, music, and spectacular parades. Picture giant, decorated floats cruising through the streets, and people dressed in feathers and glitter dancing to the rhythm of samba. It's more than a party; it's a grand showcase of art and culture!

1 Why do the mooncakes represent?
- A) The stars
- B) They symbolize unity and happiness
- C) They scare away evil spirits
- D) They are afraid of the dark

2. What is the main idea of the section titled "Colors Everywhere: The Vibrant Holi Festival"?
- A) Holi is a celebration of color and the victory of good over evil.
- B) Holi is only celebrated in spring.
- C) Colors used in Holi are made from flowers.
- D) Holi is a solemn occasion.

3. Which detail from the text supports the idea that the Day of the Dead is a celebration of remembrance?
- A) Families make altars for the departed.
- B) It's a very spooky event.
- C) People dress up in costumes.
- D) There are parades in the streets.

4. What do the words " lunar calendar" most likely mean paregraph 3?
- A) Dull
- B) Solar calendar
- C) Exciting and full of energy
- D) Moon calendar

5. From the details in the text, what can you infer about why people celebrate cultural festivals?
- A) To create chaos
- B) To honor traditions and bring communities together
- C) To compete with other countries
- D) Because they are required by law

6. How does the author make the text engaging for young readers? Please provide examples.

_____

_____

_____

_____

7. How are cultural festivals similar and different around the world? Use information from the text in your answer.

_____

_____

_____

_____

8. What are some common elements found in the cultural festivals mentioned in the text?

_____

_____

_____

_____

Write a short essay about how cultural festivals around the world can promote unity and understanding among people, using examples from the text.

_____

_____

_____

_____

_____

_____

_____

_____

_____

_____

_____

_____

_____

_____

_____

_____

_____

_____

Answer key

1 Why do the mooncakes represent?
- A) The stars
- <u>B) They symbolize unity and happiness</u>
- C) They scare away evil spirits
- D) They are afraid of the dark

2. What is the main idea of the section titled "Colors Everywhere: The Vibrant Holi Festival"?
- <u>A) Holi is a celebration of color and the victory of good over evil.</u>
- B) Holi is only celebrated in spring.
- C) Colors used in Holi are made from flowers.
- D) Holi is a solemn occasion.

3. Which detail from the text supports the idea that the Day of the Dead is a celebration of remembrance?
- <u>A) Families make altars for the departed.</u>
- B) It's a very spooky event.
- C) People dress up in costumes.
- D) There are parades in the streets.

4. What do the words " lunar calendar" most likely mean paregraph 3?
- A) Dull
- B) Solar calendar
- C) Exciting and full of energy
- <u>D) Moon calendar</u>

5. From the details in the text, what can you infer about why people celebrate cultural festivals?
- A) To create chaos
- <u>B) To honor traditions and bring communities together</u>
- C) To compete with other countries
- D) Because they are required by law

Text 4

Annotation Checklist

As you read the text, please annotate it using the following checklist:

 Underline any main ideas

 Circle any words you don't know

 Look up the words online

 Reread anything you don't understand

 Summarize after rereading

 Write Down things you find interesting

Note Taking

Name: _____

Date: _____

Recycling and Sustainability: Saving the World, One Trash Bin at a Time!

Introduction: The Superheroes of Trash

Alright, future Earth-savers, buckle up! We're diving into the world of recycling and sustainability. Now, you might be thinking, "What's so cool about old soda cans and newspapers?" Well, much like a caterpillar turning into a butterfly, recycling transforms our trash into something totally new and awesome. It's like magic, but real!

Every year, we create a mind-boggling amount of waste. Imagine a mountain of garbage so big, you can't even see the top - yikes! But here's the kicker: much of that can be recycled. When we recycle, we're being superheroes for our planet. Just like in video games, every small action can score big points for team Earth!

The Art of Recycling: More than Trash Cans

Recycling isn't just about throwing bottles and papers into a bin (though that's a part of it!). It's a whole process. First, we collect and separate our waste. This part's like a treasure hunt, sifting through things people think are no longer needed. Found a plastic bottle? Into the recycling bin it goes! What about cardboard? Yup, that too!

Next, these materials are broken down and transformed. Picture a water bottle melting down, then reshaping into a brand-new toy. Pretty neat, huh? Finally, these new products find their way back to us. We've not just reduced trash but also saved energy and resources it takes to make stuff from scratch. It's a win-win!'

Sustainability: Thinking Long-Term
Okay, so we've covered recycling, but what's the deal with sustainability? Imagine eating all your Halloween candy in one night. Sure, it's fun at first, but then you're left with a stomachache and no more treats. Sustainability is like saving some candy for later, so you can enjoy it for longer. It's about using resources in a way that doesn't ruin things for future generations.

We have to think about water, air, energy, and even animals and plants. It's like a giant jigsaw puzzle where every piece matters. If one piece goes missing, like clean water, the whole picture changes. So, we find ways to use less, waste less, and be kinder to our environment. That means turning off lights, reducing water use, and yes, recycling!

The Three R's: Reduce, Reuse, Recycle
You've probably heard about the three R's: Reduce, Reuse, and Recycle. These aren't just catchy words; they're steps to help us be more sustainable. 'Reduce' means using less stuff. You know, like choosing a big water jug at home instead of many plastic bottles. Or saying "No, thanks!" to that extra plastic bag at the store.

'Reuse' is finding new ways to use old things. That glass jar from grandma's jam? Boom, it's a new home for your pencils! 'Recycle', you're already familiar with (go, team!). But when we do all three, we're hitting sustainability's high score. It's like a triple-layer cake, with each layer adding something delicious!

Our Planet, Our Responsibility
So, why bother with all of this? Because this is our home – and we share it with millions of other living things. Every small action we do has a ripple effect, like a pebble thrown into a pond. Trash doesn't just look ugly; it can harm animals, plants, and even us (yuck!).

But there's good news: we have the power to make a change. Every bottle recycled, every light switched off, every tree planted makes a difference. And, it feels good! It's like being part of a global team, all working together to protect our world. So, let's get to it, Earth-savers!

1 What is one reason the text gives for why recycling is important?
- o A) It's a fun way to earn money
- o B) It helps protect the environment and reduces waste
- o C) It's a law that everyone has to follow
- o D) It makes our homes cleaner

2. What is the main idea of the section "Sustainability: Thinking Long-Term"?
- o A) Sustainability is about using resources wisely so they last longer.
- o B) Sustainability means using as much as we can right now.
- o C) Sustainability is the same as recycling.
- o D) Sustainability is a game played worldwide.

3. Which detail supports the idea that recycling is a process?
- o A) Recycling is just about throwing things into bins.
- o B) Used materials are collected, broken down, and transformed.
- o C) Recycling should be done once a month.
- o D) All garbage is recyclable.

4. In the context it is used, what does the word "sustainable" most likely mean?
- o A) Making a lot of noise
- o B) Using up quickly
- o C) Lasting for a long time
- o D) Being flashy and visible

5. What can be inferred about the author's opinion regarding recycling and sustainability?
- o A) They think it's unimportant.
- o B) They believe it's an individual's choice.
- o C) They find it boring and uninteresting.
- o D) They view it as essential for protecting the environment.

6. How does the author try to engage with readers about the topic of recycling and sustainability? Provide examples from the text.

_____

_____

_____

_____

7. Explain how recycling contributes to sustainability. Use information from the text in your answer.

_____

_____

_____

_____

8. What are the Three R's, and how do they help the environment?

_____

_____

_____

_____

Write an essay explaining why it's important for schools to have recycling programs. Use evidence from the text to support your answer.

_____

_____

_____

_____

_____

_____

_____

_____

_____

_____

_____

_____

_____

_____

_____

_____

Answer key

1 What is one reason the text gives for why recycling is important?

- ○ A) It's a fun way to earn money
- ○ B) It helps protect the environment and reduces waste
- ○ C) It's a law that everyone has to follow
- ○ D) It makes our homes cleaner

2. What is the main idea of the section "Sustainability: Thinking Long-Term"?

- ○ A) Sustainability is about using resources wisely so they last longer.
- ○ B) Sustainability means using as much as we can right now.
- ○ C) Sustainability is the same as recycling.
- ○ D) Sustainability is a game played worldwide.

3. Which detail supports the idea that recycling is a process?

- ○ A) Recycling is just about throwing things into bins.
- ○ B) Used materials are collected, broken down, and transformed.
- ○ C) Recycling should be done once a month.
- ○ D) All garbage is recyclable.

4. In the context it is used, what does the word "sustainable" most likely mean?

- ○ A) Making a lot of noise
- ○ B) Using up quickly
- ○ C) Lasting for a long time
- ○ D) Being flashy and visible

5. What can be inferred about the author's opinion regarding recycling and sustainability?

- ○ A) They think it's unimportant.
- ○ B) They believe it's an individual's choice.
- ○ C) They find it boring and uninteresting.
- ○ D) They view it as essential for protecting the environment.

Text 5

Annotation Checklist

As you read the text, please annotate it using the following checklist:

 Underline any main ideas

 Circle any words you don't know

 Look up the words online

 Reread anything you don't understand

 Summarize after rereading

 Write Down things you find interesting

Note Taking

Name: _____

Date: _____

Endangered Species: The Earth's Dwindling Treasures

Introduction: Nature's Needy Neighbors

Okay, friends, time to talk about something serious but in a cool way - endangered species. Imagine if, in your favorite video game, characters started disappearing and couldn't come back. Well, that's what's happening to some of the Earth's animals and plants! They're in danger of totally vanishing. But, instead of respawning, they're counting on us to save the game.

Species become endangered for various reasons like losing their homes, pollution, or even because of exotic pet trading (seriously, a tiger is NOT a house cat!). It's not just the big or cuddly ones we see in zoos; we're talking plants, insects, and all sorts of critters. Every single one is like a unique piece of art, and once they're gone, there's no getting them back.

Losing Ground: Habitat Destruction

First up on the list of troubles: habitat destruction. Imagine someone took your house, school, and favorite hangout spots, then replaced them with something else. Not cool, right? Well, when forests are cut down, oceans are polluted, or wetlands are drained, it's like someone's doing exactly that to these creatures.

Many animals need specific conditions to survive, like the panda with bamboo forests, or coral reefs for a dizzying array of marine life. When these places face destruction, it's not just an "Oopsie!" moment. It's a "We've-just-lost-a-piece-of-a-puzzle" situation, and it affects all of us, whether we see it immediately or not.

The Hunted: Poaching and Overharvesting
Now, let's chat about a super villainous activity: poaching. This isn't about cooking eggs, folks! Some people illegally hunt animals for their fur, bones, horns, or even for exotic pets. Elephants are in danger because of their ivory tusks, and rhinos for their horns. It's like taking a car's wheels while saying, "But it still has a motor!"

And it's not just animals; plants suffer too! Overharvesting happens when too many plants are taken from their wild homes, like when people over-pick medicinal plants from a forest. It's like taking all the cookies from the jar and not leaving any for your friends. No plants, no animals, no balance, no fun.

Climate Change: A Storm on the Horizon
Alright, here's a biggie: climate change. Imagine wearing a snowsuit in the desert. Sounds crazy uncomfortable, right? Well, that's how animals feel when their environments change too quickly. Rising temperatures, melting ice caps, more intense storms, and weird weather patterns? It's a lot to deal with!

Animals like polar bears, sea turtles, and even butterflies are struggling to adapt. It's not just about finding a new zip code; many can't survive the new weather or find enough food. It's like suddenly finding out your kitchen only serves spicy food, but you can't handle the heat!

Conservation Heroes: Every Bit Helps

But it's not all doom and gloom! There are conservation heroes out there, and you can join the league! Scientists, rangers, and even everyday folks are working to fix things. They create protected areas, fight against poaching, plant new forests, and clean up beaches and rivers. It's a global effort, like the biggest group project ever!

Each of us can help in small ways. Learning and teaching others about endangered species, raising money for conservation groups, or creating habitats in our own backyards. Remember, it's not just about saving them; it's about preserving the wonder and balance of the world we all share.

1 According to the text, why are some species endangered?
- A) They want new homes.
- B) They're hiding from scientists.
- C) They face threats like habitat destruction and poaching.
- D) They're moving to other planets.

2. What is the main idea of the section "Losing Ground: Habitat Destruction"?
- A) Animals willingly leave their habitats.
- B) Habitat destruction removes necessary resources and disrupts animal lives.
- C) Building new cities is good for wildlife.
- D) Pollution is a myth.

3. Which detail from the text explains a consequence of overharvesting?
- A) Animals enjoy the extra space.
- B) Plants and animals lose their balance in the ecosystem.
- C) It makes forests look prettier.
- D) Overharvesting helps plants grow better.

4. What does the term "conservation" most likely mean in the text?
- A) Wasting resources
- B) Protecting and preserving natural resources
- C) Studying in a library
- D) Starting a fire

5. How does the author view poaching?
- A) It's a noble profession.
- B) It's necessary for animal population control.
- C) It's a harmful and illegal activity.
- D) It's unrelated to endangered species.

6. How does the author try to inspire action towards helping endangered species? Provide examples from the text.

_____

_____

_____

_____

7. Why is habitat conservation important for the survival of endangered species? Use information from the text in your answer.

_____

_____

_____

_____

8. What are some actions mentioned that could help conserve endangered species?

_____

_____

_____

_____

Write an essay about the role of climate change in the endangerment of species, using examples from the text to support your points.

_____

_____

_____

_____

_____

_____

_____

_____

_____

_____

_____

_____

_____

_____

_____

_____

_____

_____

_____

Answer key

1 According to the text, why are some species endangered?
- A) They want new homes.
- B) They're hiding from scientists.
- C) They face threats like habitat destruction and poaching.
- D) They're moving to other planets.

2. What is the main idea of the section "Losing Ground: Habitat Destruction"?
- A) Animals willingly leave their habitats.
- B) Habitat destruction removes necessary resources and disrupts animal lives.
- C) Building new cities is good for wildlife.
- D) Pollution is a myth.

3. Which detail from the text explains a consequence of overharvesting?
- A) Animals enjoy the extra space.
- B) Plants and animals lose their balance in the ecosystem.
- C) It makes forests look prettier.
- D) Overharvesting helps plants grow better.

4. What does the term "conservation" most likely mean in the text?
- A) Wasting resources
- B) Protecting and preserving natural resources
- C) Studying in a library
- D) Starting a fire

5. How does the author view poaching?
- A) It's a noble profession.
- B) It's necessary for animal population control.
- C) It's a harmful and illegal activity.
- D) It's unrelated to endangered species.

Text 6

Annotation Checklist

As you read the text, please annotate it using the following checklist:

 Underline any main ideas

 Circle any words you don't know

 Look up the words online

 Reread anything you don't understand

 Summarize after rereading

 Write Down things you find interesting

 yes!

Note Taking

Early Civilizations: The Cool Kids of History!

Introduction: Way Back When, They Began!
BOOM! That's the sound of the first civilizations popping up on Earth like popcorn. But these weren't kernels, they were people! Early civilizations started sprouting up thousands of years ago, but they didn't have smartphones, cars, or even pizza! Can you imagine? These folks were living in what we call the Bronze Age, which doesn't mean everything was made of bronze, but there was definitely a lot of that metal hanging around.

These early civilizations were like the cool kids of ancient history, starting trends, creating languages, and building cities out of nothing but their bare hands, some tools, and a whole heap of determination. So, let's dust off our time-traveling gear and take a look at how these ancient trendsetters rocked the world!

Mesopotamia: The Land Between Two Rivers
First stop, Mesopotamia, aka the "Land Between Two Rivers" because it was squished right between the Tigris and Euphrates Rivers. Clever name, right? This place is now known as Iraq. But back in the day, it was home to a bunch of different groups, including the Sumerians, Akkadians, Babylonians, and Assyrians. Talk about a packed house!

Here's a fun fact: the wheel was first invented in Mesopotamia! And no, we're not just talking about a fun carnival ride. We mean the kind of wheel that's probably on your bike or skateboard. These folks also came up with one of the world's first writing systems, cuneiform, which was a lot of tiny wedge-shaped marks that make emojis seem boring!

Ancient Egypt: More Than Just Pyramids
Next up, Ancient Egypt, the land of pharaohs, mummies, and - you guessed it - pyramids! These guys weren't building triangles just because they liked the shape; these were tombs for their kings and queens. And let's not forget the Sphinx, a giant lion with a human head that was so cool, it didn't need a body!

But pyramids and Sphinxes weren't the only awesome things about Ancient Egypt. They also had hieroglyphs, which were their version of emojis, but way more complicated. They invented papyrus, sort of like ancient paper, so they deserve some serious high-fives for helping people write stuff down!

Indus Valley: The Grid-System Geniuses
Okay, let's jet over to the Indus Valley Civilization, around present-day Pakistan and northwest India. These folks were neat freaks and organization wizards! They had cities like Harappa and Mohenjo-Daro, which were so well-planned, they make your school look like it was put together last minute. We're talking about a grid system, uniform buildings, and plumbing! Yes, they had toilets!

They were also pretty mysterious because we haven't cracked their script, so we don't know what they were writing about. Maybe jokes, shopping lists, or their own version of text messages like "BRB, inventing civilization."

Ancient China: Dynasties and Dragons
Last but not least, let's swing by Ancient China. Now, these guys were all about dynasties, which are like a family holding the championship title for ruling, except the game lasts for centuries. The Xia, Shang, and Zhou Dynasties were like the all-stars of their time.

They may not have invented pizza, but they did come up with something equally mind-blowing: paper! Like, actual paper, which makes them the grandparents of books, money, and homework. They also rocked at poetry, philosophy, and public works. And they loved dragons, not the fire-breathing kind, but as a symbol of power and good luck!

1 What invention from Mesopotamia does the text mention is still used today?
- A) Smartphones
- B) Pyramids
- C) The wheel
- D) Dragons

2. What is the main idea of the section about Ancient Egypt?
- A) It focuses only on pyramids.
- B) Hieroglyphs were simple drawings.
- C) Ancient Egypt was known for various contributions and unique structures.
- D) The Sphinx was the most important invention.

3. Which detail from the text supports the main idea of the "Indus Valley" section?
- A) They had the first form of emojis.
- B) Cities like Harappa and Mohenjo-Daro were well-planned.
- C) The Indus Valley Civilization was messy.
- D) They built the Sphinx.

4. What does the word "dynasties" mean in the context of the "Ancient China" section?
- A) Types of dragons
- B) Paper inventions
- C) Family lines that rule for many years
- D) Well-planned cities

5. Why does the author refer to early civilizations as the "cool kids of history"?
- A) They all lived in cold climates.
- B) They were trendy and made significant contributions.
- C) They had modern technology.
- D) They were all young.

6. How does the author's choice of language make the text more interesting for young readers? Provide examples.

_____

_____

_____

_____

7. Why were the cities of the Indus Valley Civilization considered well-planned? Use information from the text in your answer.

_____

_____

_____

_____

8. What were some contributions of Ancient civilizations mentioned in the text?

_____

_____

_____

_____

Write an essay about the importance of studying early civilizations, using details from the text to support your points.

_____

_____

_____

_____

_____

_____

_____

_____

_____

_____

_____

_____

_____

_____

_____

_____

_____

_____

_____

Answer key

1 What invention from Mesopotamia does the text mention is still used today?
- A) Smartphones
- B) Pyramids
- C) The wheel
- D) Dragons

2. What is the main idea of the section about Ancient Egypt?
- A) It focuses only on pyramids.
- B) Hieroglyphs were simple drawings.
- C) Ancient Egypt was known for various contributions and unique structures.
- D) The Sphinx was the most important invention.

3. Which detail from the text supports the main idea of the "Indus Valley" section?
- A) They had the first form of emojis.
- B) Cities like Harappa and Mohenjo-Daro were well-planned.
- C) The Indus Valley Civilization was messy.
- D) They built the Sphinx.

4. What does the word "dynasties" mean in the context of the "Ancient China" section?
- A) Types of dragons
- B) Paper inventions
- C) Family lines that rule for many years
- D) Well-planned cities

5. Why does the author refer to early civilizations as the "cool kids of history"?
- A) They all lived in cold climates.
- B) They were trendy and made significant contributions.
- C) They had modern technology.
- D) They were all young.

Text 7

Annotation Checklist

As you read the text, please annotate it using the following checklist:

 Underline any main ideas

 Circle any words you don't know

 Look up the words online

 Reread anything you don't understand

 Summarize after rereading

 Write Down things you find interesting

Note Taking

The 7 Wonders of the World: Earth's Cool Collection!

Introduction: What's the Wonder?

Hey, wonder buddies! Ever heard of the Seven Wonders of the World? No, they're not superheroes, but they're super cool! They're like the Earth's trophy case, showing off the most jaw-dropping, eye-popping places humans have made. From giant statues to massive tombs, these wonders had people of ancient times saying "WOW!" just like we do when we nail a video game on the hardest level.

Now, here's a shocker: most of these wonders aren't standing anymore! Yep, it's a bummer. But don't worry, their stories are still with us, and they're as awesome as a triple-chocolate sundae. So, let's dive into history's scrapbook and flip through the pages of these ancient marvels.

And remember, these aren't just old rocks; they're a blast from the past, showing us what people can do with some creativity, hard work, and a whole lot of "We CAN do this!"

The Great Pyramid of Giza: A Desert Dream

First up, the only wonder still kicking it with us today: the Great Pyramid of Giza. This pyramid is like the world's oldest skyscraper, but, you know, without the glass and elevators.

Built as a massive tomb in Egypt, it's been hanging around for about 4,500 years. That's older than your great-great-great-(a lot of greats)-grandparents!

The pyramid was made for a pharaoh named Khufu. But here's the fun part: it wasn't built by aliens or magical creatures but by thousands of super skilled workers. And they didn't have fancy machines or robots; they used their brains, muscles, and some pretty nifty ancient tools.

Standing tall at 481 feet, it was the tallest man-made structure for over 3,800 years! Imagine stacking around 200 giraffes on top of each other. Yep, that tall! It's like the ancient world's version of a world record.

Hanging Gardens of Babylon: A Lush Legend
Next, let's imagine a place so green and lush you'd think you stepped into a fairy tale. Welcome to the Hanging Gardens of Babylon! Now, spoiler alert: we're not even sure if they ever existed. If they did, they're long gone, and we don't have pictures (cameras weren't a thing back then). But the stories? Pure gold.

Legend has it that King Nebuchadnezzar II built the gardens for his homesick wife, who missed her green, mountainous homeland. These weren't just any old gardens. They were a mountain of terraces with all sorts of trees and flowers, and they were built in the desert! How? The Babylonians were master engineers who came up with ingenious ways to water the plants.

They say the gardens were a sight to behold, a green dream in the heart of a bustling city. It shows that love can move mountains, or in this case, build them!

Statue of Zeus at Olympia: A Thunderous Wonder

Imagine walking into a temple and seeing a statue so tall it felt like it could wear the roof as a hat! That was the Statue of Zeus at Olympia. Created by the sculptor Phidias in ancient Greece, this statue was... wait for it... 40 feet tall! That's like stacking about eight cars on top of each other.

Zeus sat on a fancy throne, all made of gold and ivory. It wasn't just big; it was shiny! People came from far and wide just to catch a glimpse. It was like the ancient version of a celebrity photo op.

Sadly, like the fate of a lost balloon, the statue didn't stick around. It was eventually destroyed, but not before leaving a mark as one of the most famous artworks of the ancient world.

The Rest of the Wonders: A Quick Tour

Phew! Visiting four wonders is exciting but exhausting! Let's speed-run through the last three. The Temple of Artemis at Ephesus: a huge temple dedicated to the goddess Artemis, complete with super tall columns. The Mausoleum at Halicarnassus: a monumental tomb built for Mausolus, a Persian governor, which was so awesome that 'mausoleum' became the word for grand tombs! And finally, the Colossus of Rhodes: a ginormous statue of the sun god Helios, which greeted ships entering the harbor.

And let's not forget the Lighthouse of Alexandria, the world's first lighthouse! It helped sailors find their way, proving that even back then, people were thinking about safety first.

Though most of these wonders are lost to time, their legacies live on. They remind us of the incredible things humans can achieve and inspire us to reach for our very own stars.

1 According to the text, how many of the original Seven Wonders still exist today?
- A) Four
- B) Seven
- C) One
- D) None

2. What is the main idea of the section "The Great Pyramid of Giza: A Desert Dream"?
- A) The Great Pyramid is a mystery nobody understands.
- B) The Great Pyramid was built with advanced technology.
- C) The Great Pyramid is the oldest of the wonders and was a remarkable human achievement.
- D) The Great Pyramid was created for agricultural purposes.

3. Which detail supports the idea that the Hanging Gardens were special?
- A) They were the only gardens in Babylon.
- B) They were a mountain of terraces with various plants in the desert.
- C) They were easy to build.
- D) They are well-documented with photographs.

4. In the text, what does the word "ingenious" most likely mean?
- A) Silly
- B) Complicated
- C) Clever or inventive
- D) Useless

5. What is the author's purpose in describing the size of the wonders using familiar objects?
- A) To confuse readers
- B) To make the text longer
- C) To help readers understand and visualize their scale
- D) To show that the wonders are overrated

6. How does the author make the information about the Seven Wonders engaging?

_____

_____

_____

_____

7. Why do you think the Seven Wonders of the World are still remembered and discussed today?

_____

_____

_____

_____

8. What were some of the materials used in the construction of the Statue of Zeus at Olympia?

_____

_____

_____

_____

Write an essay explaining why the Great Pyramid of Giza has survived when the other Wonders haven't. Explain why it is such a marvel to look at. Use information from the text to support your points.

_____

_____

_____

_____

_____

_____

_____

_____

_____

_____

_____

_____

_____

_____

_____

_____

_____

_____

Answer key

1 According to the text, how many of the original Seven Wonders still exist today?

- A) Four
- B) Seven
- C) One
- D) None

2. What is the main idea of the section "The Great Pyramid of Giza: A Desert Dream"?

- A) The Great Pyramid is a mystery nobody understands.
- B) The Great Pyramid was built with advanced technology.
- C) The Great Pyramid is the oldest of the wonders and was a remarkable human achievement.
- D) The Great Pyramid was created for agricultural purposes.

3. Which detail supports the idea that the Hanging Gardens were special?

- A) They were the only gardens in Babylon.
- B) They were a mountain of terraces with various plants in the desert.
- C) They were easy to build.
- D) They are well-documented with photographs.

4. In the text, what does the word "ingenious" most likely mean?

- A) Silly
- B) Complicated
- C) Clever or inventive
- D) Useless

5. What is the author's purpose in describing the size of the wonders using familiar objects?

- A) To confuse readers
- B) To make the text longer
- C) To help readers understand and visualize their scale
- D) To show that the wonders are overrated

Text 8

Annotation Checklist

As you read the text, please annotate it using the following checklist:

- ☑ Underline any main ideas
- ☑ Circle any words you don't know
- ☑ Look up the words online
- ☑ Reread anything you don't understand
- ☑ Summarize after rereading
- ☑ Write Down things you find interesting

yes!

Note Taking

Name: _____

Date: _____

Polar Animals and Adaptation: Chillin' with the Coolest Critters on Earth!

Introduction: A Cold Welcome

Brrr! Is it just me, or did it suddenly get chilly in here? Oh, wait! We're just heading to the coldest places on Earth—the Polar Regions! Imagine your freezer, but, like, a million times bigger and with no ice cream. Sad, I know. But, hey! It's home to some of the coolest (get it?) animals you'll ever meet. And guess what? They don't even need jackets. Let's slide (maybe on our bellies like penguins) into the icy world of polar animals and their mind-blowing adaptations!

Polar Bear-y Cold: Kings and Queens of the Arctic

First stop, the Arctic, where polar bears reign supreme! They're like the fluffy giants of the North, but don't let their cuddly looks fool you. These beasts are fierce! You think surviving a week of school without your phone is tough? Try living on floating ice where it's darker than inside a sealed cookie jar for six months of the year.

Polar bears have wicked cool adaptations. Their white fur isn't just fabulous; it's camouflage, baby! And it's not actually white —it's transparent and hollow, trapping the sun's heat. Under that fur, their skin is black, soaking up even more warmth! Plus, their fat layer is thicker than a triple-decker sandwich, keeping them toasty.

Penguins: Waddling Wonders of the South Pole

A hop, skip, and a really long jump from the Arctic, and we're with the penguins in Antarctica! No, they don't live with polar bears (they'd be a tasty snack!). These birds are oddballs, trading flight for flippers and air for icy water. Imagine choosing to swim in a frozen pool every day. That's hardcore!

Penguins have their own set of adaptations. They wear a tuxedo all day, not because they're fancy, but for camouflage while swimming. Their wings work like turbo flippers, and their bodies are fuselage, designed to torpedo through the water after fish.

But the coolest thing? They huddle! Like, all the time. It's a massive cuddle party, sharing warmth. Aww!

Seals and Walruses: Slick and Skilled Survivors

Back to the Arctic (pack your imaginary mittens!), and let's chat about seals and their humongous cousins, walruses. These slippery customers are experts at life in water and on land—kind of like if your bathtub was also your bed... that sounds more splashy than comfy, huh?

Seals and walruses have blubber, a thick layer of fat (nope, they're not just big-boned) that keeps them warm in icy waters. They can also slow their heartbeat and push blood away from their skin in cold water, making them super divers!

Walruses go the extra mile with long tusks that help them poke holes in the ice for breathing or haul their hefty bodies out of the water. Talk about multi-tools!

Conclusion: The Chill Life
Who knew the coldest places on Earth were jam-packed with such cool residents? From polar bears to penguins to walruses, these animals have adaptation on lock. They're not just surviving; they're THRIVING, rocking out their unique features like superstars.

So, the next time you're feeling a bit chilly, remember our polar pals. They've turned the big freeze into the cool place to be, with a side of survival skills that are off the charts. Stay cool, friends!

1. What is an adaptation that helps polar bears stay warm?
   - A) Their fur changes colors.
   - B) Their white fur traps the sun's heat and their skin is black.
   - C) They huddle together.
   - D) They migrate to warmer areas.
2. What is the main idea of the section "Penguins: Waddling Wonders of the South Pole"?
   - A) Penguins struggle to survive in the cold.
   - B) Penguins fly from the Arctic to the Antarctic.
   - C) Penguins have unique adaptations for life in icy water.
   - D) Penguins are the primary prey of polar bears.
3. Which detail from the text best supports the main idea that walruses have specific adaptations to thrive in their environment?
   - A) Walruses are found only in the Arctic.
   - B) Walruses use their tusks to help them breathe and move onto the ice.
   - C) Walruses and seals are cousins.
   - D) Walruses are larger than seals.
4. What does the word "fuselage" likely mean in the passage?
   - A) Old and broken
   - B) Perfectly shaped for flying
   - C) Perfectly shaped for moving through water
   - D) Loud and noisy
5. Why does the author use a humorous and casual style in the passage?
   - A) To make fun of polar animals
   - B) To confuse readers about the facts
   - C) To engage readers and make complex information more relatable
   - D) To show that the topic is not serious

6. Explain how the author's writing style helps to convey information about animal adaptations. What is the tone, style, etc?

_____

_____

_____

_____

7. Why are adaptations crucial for animals living in Polar Regions?

_____

_____

_____

_____

8. How do penguins keep warm according to the passage?

_____

_____

_____

_____

Write an essay on how the physical characteristics of polar animals help them survive in extreme cold conditions. Use information from the text to support your explanation.

_____

_____

_____

_____

_____

_____

_____

_____

_____

_____

_____

_____

_____

_____

_____

_____

_____

_____

Answer key

1. What is an adaptation that helps polar bears stay warm?
    - A) Their fur changes colors.
    - <u>B) Their white fur traps the sun's heat and their skin is black.</u>
    - C) They huddle together.
    - D) They migrate to warmer areas.
2. What is the main idea of the section "Penguins: Waddling Wonders of the South Pole"?
    - A) Penguins struggle to survive in the cold.
    - B) Penguins fly from the Arctic to the Antarctic.
    - <u>C) Penguins have unique adaptations for life in icy water.</u>
    - D) Penguins are the primary prey of polar bears.
3. Which detail from the text best supports the main idea that walruses have specific adaptations to thrive in their environment?
    - A) Walruses are found only in the Arctic.
    - <u>B) Walruses use their tusks to help them breathe and move onto the ice.</u>
    - C) Walruses and seals are cousins.
    - D) Walruses are larger than seals.
4. What does the word "fuselage" likely mean in the passage?
    - A) Old and broken
    - B) Perfectly shaped for flying
    - <u>C) Perfectly shaped for moving through water</u>
    - D) Loud and noisy
5. Why does the author use a humorous and casual style in the passage?
    - A) To make fun of polar animals
    - B) To confuse readers about the facts
    - <u>C) To engage readers and make complex information more relatable</u>
    - D) To show that the topic is not serious

Made in United States
Troutdale, OR
01/31/2024

17347597R00051